To Andaye from her Amazon,
friend — bloodied but unbowed!

Jenny
x

When I Became an Amazon

A Poetry Sequence
Jenny Lewis
Illustrations
Tinker Mather

IRON PRESS

First published 1996 by IRON Press
5 Marden Terrace, Cullercoats
North Shields, Northumberland, NE30 4PD, UK
Tel/Fax: (0191) 253 1901

Second print 1997

Typeset by David Stephenson
in Palatino 11 point

Printed by Peterson Printers
South Shields

Illustrations by Tinker Mather

Cover and book design by Peter Mortimer

ISBN 0 906228 60 3

IRON Press books are represented by:
Password Books Ltd.
23 New Mount Street
Manchester M4 4DE
Tel: (0161) 953 4009
Fax: (0161) 953 4001

To my mother, Kathleen Rosa Lewis, 1903 – 1974.

Acknowledgements

I'd like to thank some of the many people whose encouragement helped me in the writing, revision and editing of this book. My sister, Gillian Beetham, and my friends Frances Kiernan, Angy Man and Elspeth Sandys; Peter Mortimer of IRON, and Keiren Phelan of Southern Arts whose support has been much appreciated.

By the same author (under the name Jenny Hawkesworth):

The Lonely Skyscraper (Walker Books, 1981)
A Handbook of Family Monsters (Dent 1982)
Me and My Dinosaur (Polka Children's Theatre, 1988)

Jenny Lewis

studied at the Ruskin School of Art, Oxford, and lived in Yorkshire for 13 years where she wrote children's books. *A Handbook of Family Monsters*, published by J. M. Dent, 1982, featured a national Invent-a-Monster Competition judged by Michael Palin and Terry Jones of Monty Python, with results published in Quarto magazine. She ran Creative Writing workshops for MIND in Harrogate and collaborated on *Fat Pig - The Musical* at the Leicester Haymarket Theatre, 1987. In 1988, she wrote a children's musical, *Me and*  *My Dinosaur*, for the Polka Children's Theatre, Wimbledon. She has two sons and now lives in Oxford, where she is the Poetry Society representative and Assistant Editor of IRON magazine. She is presently completing a major commission from Coral Arts to write a poetry cycle - *The Gifts of the Angels* - to be performed at Dorchester Abbey in October, 1996.

Tinker Mather

studied at Liverpool College of Art and, after raising four children, worked as full-time artist and teacher. She was a founder member of the Oxford Artists Group. She taught in Oxford for ten years and then became a visiting lecturer in the U.S.A. She was subsequently awarded a Travel Scholarship to India where she lectured in Santiniketan, Baroda and Calcutta Universities. She has exhibited in Nairobi, Calcutta, Bonn, Brussels, Paris and London. Her work has been used for book covers by Isis, Women's Art, Virago  and Cambridge University Presses. She has been through breast cancer and come out on the other side, since when writing has taken over from painting. Her poetry has been published in the Guardian, the Independent, IRON magazine and Pyramid Press.

Author and Illustrator photographs by Nutz

Preface

The Modern Woman

In March 1985, a pea-sized lump in my right breast was diagnosed as cancer. Within days I was admitted to hospital and had first a lumpectomy, then a radical mastectomy. I was told I might have only months, or even weeks, to live. My sons were aged eleven and six. Among the many letters and cards I received one was from a friend who wrote "Dear Jenny – now you are a true Amazon." At a time of terror, confusion and chaos, it made me smile and it put me in touch with a part of myself that was determined to survive.

In the intervening years, I thought a lot about the Amazons and about how, for modern women, the powerful, outward-going energies of our tribal ancestresses are often subverted to the whims of a patriarchal culture in which women have been taught to feel shame for their sexuality and distaste for female behaviour which is non-submissive. So we turn our energies inwards which leads to depression, chronic unhappiness and, ultimately, an erosion of the immune system which leaves us defenceless against diseases such as cancer.

At the time of writing this I am, luckily, still in remission from cancer. My children are now 23 and 17. With the help of friends, family, therapy and some kind and supportive doctors, I was able to find the courage to change my life to one with which I felt comfortable. So I now have an infinitely better chance of survival.

The Amazon

Eighteen months ago, a neighbour handed me a cutting from the Daily Telegraph reporting recent discoveries of massed graves of Iron Age warrior women buried with their armour and weapons in Southern Russia, with iron arrow-heads embedded in their skeletons. They could have been Scythian women who fought alongside their menfolk. Or they could have been, as a growing number of Western academics are beginning to believe, a separate phenomenon – a tribe of nomadic female warriors who roamed the steppe around 700-500 BC. If this is so, theirs was likely to have been a horse culture and they would have used turkish-style bows in battle. In order to draw their bows easily, they would almosrt certainly have bound one breast down with a wide leather strap – as is the custom of modern women archers – making them appear one-breasted. Just such a tribe of fighting women, in fact, on which the mythical Amazons might have been based.

Inspired by this knowledge, I began to write a poetry cycle in which I combined details from my reading about Iron Age tribes in Southern Russia and the Mediterranean with scraps of conflicting information about the Amazons drawn from the Greek myths. I counterpointed the result with my own experience. *When I Became an Amazon* isn't intended to be historically or biographically accurate but rather to provide a dramatic context for a poem in which the power and courage of women is celebrated; and in which their story, for a change, is unequivocally centre stage.

Jenny Lewis
Oxford, Summer 1996

———————

The story is told in three voices:-

THE AMAZON, OREITHYIA

THE SHAMAN, FATHER OF OREITHYIA

THE MODERN WOMAN

When I
Became an
Amazon

Prologue

When I became an Amazon
I consulted the warrior priestess
in me, who had been sleeping.
She told me to take up my weapons
of poetry, wisdom and purity of intention
that I had put away as a young girl
for the sake of being loved by men.

THE AMAZON

There were twelve of us
in that desert town,
under a sky dark as grape bloom,
with belts of flying stars to guide us
back to where our mothers waited
to garland us with wreaths of oleander.

They too had been tested in their time.
They too, rallying strength from tired
sinews, just like us after the long
mosquito-bothering days – our palms
branded by the hot metal of javelins.

We ran naked and the townspeople
came in droves to watch us.
Our bodies glinted like spears.
Our shaved heads were globes
of light reflecting our pride.
In each ear a precious ring had
told us from birth that we too
were precious.

As we entered the stadium, the roar
of wonder that greeted us was like
fire consuming the mountain.
This was what it had all been for.
The weeks of running without respite
up sharp tracks that cut our feet
to the bone. Meeting only goats
with marbly eyes the colour of urine,
or wild cats that swore at us
from a safe distance.

Sometimes we swam in icy rivers,
battling the steely curves of the torrent
for survival. And some of us didn't survive –
but there was no grieving for the lost;
except the mother was allowed
one hour at sunset for a final leave-taking
to be alone. But tears were not permitted.
Tears were only for men and babies.

When I was a small child, visiting my mother
Hippolyta's tent at evening as she drew up plans
for the next great battles – she told me I must
go forward straight as a spear thrust, fast as
sling-shot. To always go forward proudly –
her true and only daughter Oreithyia.

Then she went away, leading the great, rolling war
chariots. And we were left watching the horizon,
counting the hours and days, realising that waiting
can be the real torture. The nights were worst.

I made little cakes and laid them with flowers
at the altar of Artemis for her safe return.
And I kept her tent tidy – polishing her trophies,
arranging and re-arranging her jewelled pendants
and bracelets. Loving her quietly in her absence.

By day I hunted with my father in the forest.
Learning to fish in the hardest part of the river;
building light rafts for shooting the rapids; riding
bareback on the keenest horses, clinging low
to their necks with manes and hair flying.

At seven I learned to use arrows and javelins.
A year later, by wielding my axe I could behead
a rabbit at twenty paces. By nine I could live
for days on my own away from the camp.

I learned to blend with the trees and bushes;
stay still as a stoat with only the tremor
of pulse under skin connecting me to the living
skin of the earth and leaves. At fourteen,
they chose me for my speed and agility to compete
in the games. So I left my father and travelled
many months over seas and mountains and on
into the dry mouth of the desert to prove myself.

We flew over the hurdles like angels –
stretching the gap between leaders
and followers inexorably. It was always
us out in front, always, our bronze forms
glowing like embers, fired by a violent,
unquenchable energy that seemed to
transform air into our natural element,
reconnecting us with dull earth only
for the brief, sandy thud of foot on
ground in the one two three four pulsing
rhythm that drummed in our blood
as we raced in heart, mind and body
towards the glorious finish.

They rose in bellowing ranks to cheer us.
Human mountains, tottering and waving,
with children held shoulder high to glimpse
us speeding past. And some at the bottom
crushed dead by the crowd's weight.
And still they came pouring into the city
like ants, hundreds and thousands of them
day after burning day. And all of this so they
could say – I saw them, I was there.

I saw the Amazons.

THE MODERN WOMAN
Premonition
10th March, 1985

You found it first –
That night you touched me
with nerve endings like your finest paintbrush
sending a wash of sunrise through me,
flooding with luminous brilliance the misty
landscapes I never dreamt existed –

the love I felt before seemed dim
as candlelight beside those deep webs
of radiance, showing me peaceful contours
lit by intense morning and evening colours
like falls of silk over mountains.

Only you have met the warrior-priestess
in me, at once your primeval lover
and arch enemy – she stands by our side
in battle helping us draw up lines
for the next hundred thousand millenia.

She made me see – it wasn't how much
you loved me that mattered,
but how much love
you showed me I was capable of.
That was your gift – why you alone
could come inside the inner sanctum.

Later you told me what your lips
had found already, and kissing my breast
goodbye, you held me to your body
to block out the darkness of centuries;
but by daylight you had left and I was
bitterly alone - that night you touched me.

THE AMAZON

At birth they touched our right breasts
with a scorching brand to stunt growth;
and we accepted this – needing freedom,
when we grew, to draw our bows
and smoothly loose our iron-tipped arrows.

Every other part of us was concerned
with winning. Legs powering us to the front.
Arms and shoulders hurling javelins –
swinging the discus in rhythmic arcs;
and the epicentre just below the coccyx
from where we drew our strength for shot put.

All worked together like a well trained whole.
We agreed, you need only one breast
to feed a baby and saw the mutilation
as our badge of honour; the fierce sacrifice
we make that binds us to our vows,
that wakes us to our purpose; to survive,
to overcome, to come home.

We travelled home across the giant skulls
of frost-capped mountains, scrambling with our
mules up rocky cheekbones, sleeping at night
in bony sockets lined with moss and bracken.

We bought kif from shepherds to smoke round
the campfire. Slowly the winding shadows
of the desert receded from our minds and we looked
forwards to the sea voyage; to the vast, treeless plains
and pleasures of homecoming carrying trophies.

One evening we stopped by a lake which mirrored
tops of mountains dipped, as it seemed, in molten
colours that flowed, intensified, shone and cooled
first gold then amber, amethyst, mauve, lavender,
hyacinth; rose pinks fading to light, delicate greens
and yellows smudged with the first tinge of darkness.

Then we stood at the edge of mysterious night,
awed by the majesty and loneliness of those far spaces
echoing with stars. The stillness called us with tidal voices.
We heard the oceans breathing in and out on unseen
shores; and when a rush of wind catching the sails

of giant oaks in sleeping forests, turning the world
slowly towards morning, blew cold and strong
against our faces, we joined hands with our sisters
through the ages, welcoming their knowledge gathered
from the depths of the universe. And we felt the thin thread
of pain in its burning pathway, linking us century after century.

THE MODERN WOMAN
Doctor
20th March, 1985

*As he talks his hands jump in and out
of his pockets, square hands,
brave with the exact science
of mending faulty instruments.
(And the pain of his knife
is like violin strings breaking.)*

*His white coat gives him immunity
against our germs, and griefs –
our women's longings for love, babies
and healthy breast tissue.*

*All we want is the right answer.
Pecking after facts, ignorant as hens,
eyes small with hope, only half digesting
what he says. All that technical data
so patiently explained, falls before us
in a sombre harvest to be winnowed blindly
for the magic words – 'non fatal'.*

*But instead he tells me I am the one in twelve.
He cannot say how long I have to live
until the results of further tests come.*

*To the eleven others life is more benign.
They touch his hand, weeping with gratitude.
Then he turns his head away to avoid my eyes
which plead 'save me'.*

*And people come with unwanted gifts
of comfort and pity.*

Becoming an Amazon
23rd March, 1985

So I am left alone to face the night
with only a glowing ceiling eye to watch me,
like Charon, awaiting his passenger.
Shiny patches on the white metal cabinets
look like maps of desert islands
when I half close my eyes.
I long to escape and find the sun,
far away from this grim country
where fear and death
gather like stagnant pools
on harsh, ancient leaves.

The wildness calls me with primal voices
but is it asking me to leave – or come home?

Mother
24th March, 1985

*What I need is a warm, living goddess
to pray to, not a dark, forbidding father
or some poor, dead man nailed to a tree
and joined with me in being a victim.*

*Where is she? My tall, long-limbed,
golden-haired, beautiful mother
who smelled of chiffon scarves and the
Elizabeth Arden face powder she kept
in a cut glass bowl on the dressing table
under a huge blue powder puff.*

*Each day she set her morning face
towards the world of business
where she daily matched the tasks
of Heracles, on the third floor
of a small, suburban department store.*

*And as she toiled among the fashion suits
and knitwear we took turns to tend her shrine,
polishing her mirrors and dressing table;
spending inordinate hours arranging
and re-arranging the little glass and china*

*animals on her mantelpiece; setting vases
of freesias and lilies-of-the-valley carefully
on the newly shined surface of her bedside
table, loving her quietly in her absence.*

*Her memory still lives – vivid and powerful;
humming the vibrant energies of generations
of mothers.The ancestor force, oceanic
and mountainous, yet fine as grass ends
feeling the sky with delicate fingers,
blindly sensing the right way forward.*

THE SHAMAN

When I became the father of an Amazon I was set apart from men
content to follow ordinary lives in service to this great race
of warriors – as craftsmen, carpenters, midwives, domestics.

If Hippolyta hadn't chosen me to be the father of her royal child
I would have stayed quietly in the forest, living on nature's charity;
a holy man, avoiding the pain of life. Avoiding, certainly, my
sickness

and horror when Hippolyta was captured by our Greek enemies;
and then the long years of waiting at home as our daughter
mounted
campaign after campaign to defeat Theseus and bring her mother
back to us.

Yes, I could have escaped all this but then also escaped love and as
a result
been cold and barbarous like the Greeks who despise women. Yet it
was two
women who made me see how much love I was capable of - my
lover

Hippolyta and our child, Oreithyia.From childhood I'd had the gift
of visions – been able to interpret signs, stones falling at random;
patterns made by the birds, like handfuls of grain flung up against
the sky.

I understood the shape and colour of sheeps' bones; I heard rocks
and trees
resonate with their own wisdom. But on returning from the
wars having killed three enemies and entitled to take her first lover,

the young Hipployta chose me. I remember the heat of the day,
and the green river shadows – how I reached out to steady her horse
as it lost its footing down the bank. I remember how her smile

caught the sun like a shield; how at the ceremony she walked the lines
until she found me. They placed a hide cape with horsetail fringes
round my shoulders; and round my waist a red woven girdle to show

my new nobility, then led me inside to a couch where I inhaled fumes
of cannabis to cleanse and prepare my spirit for the night to come.
In the firelight outside the tent, the singing, drinking, dancing and revelry

went on until night fall. At last it was time, and my friends walked in silence
with me through the fields of our childhood, bringing me to the holy
meeting place where fate with open hand stood ready to greet us.

After the victory ceremony, they rubbed us with
perfumed oil and gave us Greek wine to drink from
a silver cup. Then, making a sign on our foreheads

with ashes, they left us alone to find our way
up to the temple of Artemis. The white moon
flooded the landscape with ghostly brilliance;

nightingales and cicadas sang from thickets
against the rushing of the stream that cooled
the sacred grove. Scents of thyme and camomile

drifted up as we trod the springy turf scattered
with olive bark and pine cones. Entering a clearing
I took Hippolyta's hand and turned her towards me

then trembling, laid her down under the moonlight,
and thrumming with a thousand buds about to burst,
I knelt and bowed my head before her intense beauty.

Queen, priestess and warrior, she was mine in the
fragrant summer night – given me by the goddess
even mightier than the god of love and anger.

Breathless, I touched her body, tracing the shadows
with fingertips light as moth wings. I was filled
with reverence and desire.When I entered her

it was like a ship entering harbour on still waters
laden with gifts of myrrh and frankincense,
perfumes from the East, shoals of flickering silver

from the sea; olive oil leaking warm from a cracked amphora,
vines heavy with grapes, their purple wine staining a white cloth;
bronze urns chased with gold made by the finest crafstmen;

fields and fields of standing corn as far as a ten day march
and then another ten and more and more; and horses red,
grey and black as night with stars like burrs caught in their pelts.

All the riches of the world I brought as tribute to this young girl.
And afterwards, she stroked my hair, kissed my hot face;
then drowsy and smiling, lay safe in my arms until sunrise.

THE MODERN WOMAN
Mother
25th March 1985

From first light, Mum was out battling the world
six days a week with a half day Wednesdays.
That was the best day, a holy day. Listening
for her key in the lock,trying not to fidget
in the warm, shadowed room after lunch
as my grandmother slept, I'd count the minutes

ticked away by the old French clock with its gilt
ornaments. It was summer; the heat and dust
of London shut out except for the blinding square
of light from the open balcony door. I closed
my eyes and thought of the pink, green
and white ice cream my mother would have

stopped to buy on the way home. Vanilla, strawberry
and pistachio – striped like a seaside awning.
But all too soon eating ice-cream with mum
would be over, and there'd be another long, grey
sock of time without her. Out in the countryside,
somewhere far away, I knew the wind was making

playful thumbprints on water, ruffling the down
on tiny bobbing ducklings.Yet in the depths,
there was an altogether more menacing world.
It was the world of drowning at enormous speed
with slip streams of river weed; of being a blind,
blue and green corpse banging senselessly

*against tree roots with tangled hair streaming
crazily, rushing through watery tunnels to shoot
far out into the boundless ocean. Often in my dreams
the river sucked me under.The current was travelling
cold, silver and fast as a bullet. There was the icy
promise of reunion with the dead. I knew my father
was waiting for me; waiting to hold me in his arms
again as he had once before at my birth.*

Understanding the Enemy
25 March 1985

I struggle to the surface, burst into daylight,
as Sister asks – "Are you awake?" She sits
on my bed, then starts holding both my hands
and looking so serious, I know the enemy
can no longer be avoided. She says quietly –
"You should prepare for the worst."

Then "Cancer often follows loss. Have you lost
someone close to you recently? Or is there
something you feel you need but you can't have?"

I tell her about my son, banished by family tradition
to prep school; and about the friend I'd like to be with
who is already father to another family. I tell her
about the rage and frustration locked deep inside me –
a Pandora's Box waiting for someone to lift the lid.

Sister recommends I let it all out.
Then she gives me a pill – the first of many –
and leaves me to my thoughts.

Loss
25th March 1985

The school trunk was his father's.
For days it stood in the hall, packed
with new shirts, socks, underpants,
* vests, shorts, pyjamas, handkerchiefs –*
all carefully labelled with the name
of an eight year old boy.

My eight year old boy.

When the trunk was gone,
the grief remained – staining
the floor and walls, washing
through the house, lapping
his empty bed, his place at table.

Others whose children had gone
away said – "It's as if they've died,
isn't it?" But all I could hear was the
patient slap of the water. And all
I could think was – "Why did I let him go?"

Something I Can't Have
30th March 1985

You come to see me one morning
with a bunch of flowers and sit looking
too big for the visitor's chair beside my bed.
You hold my hand. We smile. I bite my lip.

You tell me you knew what it was, from that
night you touched me; then you kiss me,
not caring about all the drains and drips
and tubes coming out of me. I can feel your heat

and the force fields of life surrounding you.
I feel reconnected suddenly and with a jolt
I want you — want to be with you, want your
invading energies to sweep me away,

to take me captive – provide the solution.
But nothing has changed. It is no more
possible now than it was before, cancer
or no cancer. You sigh and get up to go

back to the family who wait for you, the family
who need you as much as I do. It's an ancient
battle in which there are no winners, only potential
casualties and, if we're lucky, some survivors.

Wounded in Action
30th March, 1985

When you're gone, Matron helps me remove
the bandage, then holds me in kind, starched
arms as I register my loss in the hard stare
of the bathroom mirror – a wounded soldier
who can no longer be kissed better.

All afternoon I play Mozart loudly
on my headphones, trying to staunch
the rising tides of panic and hoist myself
to a higher plane from which it might
be easier to jump – when the time comes.

At last I hear the comforting rattle
of the tea trolley and think to myself –
"Thank God, here comes the cavalry!"

The Amazon

We rode our stallions into battle –
red, grey and black, an invincible tide
bursting the dam of the horizon,
flooding the plain with vengeful energy.

We were a young army, thirsty for fame
and glory. The rewards were great –
respect and honour from the tribe,
first pick of the best men and horses.

We could turn each horse on an acorn,
wheel 12 hundred together as one
with the ease of an eagle's shadow
gliding smoothly over the steppes.

We came within bowshot of our enemies
and loosed five or six high flights of arrows
to make them to raise their shields,
then with our famous yodelling war cry

rising over the thunder of chariots; the
crashing of iron on iron; the shrieks
of the dying and wounded, and the meagre
piping of Greek flutes – we mounted the attack.

Sometimes our womanhood was useful
as when Penthesilea fell at Troy
losing her helmet and setting free her
waving, waist-length, burnished hair.

Achilles and his Greeks stood silent –
gaping at her beauty though her face
was smeared with mud and sweat.
So we disarmed them, using the spell

our sister cast in death to our advantage.
But in a later battle we were betrayed by my aunt
Antiope's weakness for Theseus, and routed,
we returned to our Scythian homelands.

My mother, Hippolyta, mounted a campaign
to rescue Antiope and was herself captured.
Then I, Oreithyia raised twenty thousand troops
of Amazons and Scythians. We moved in dead

of winter over the earth's frozen face through Thrace,
Thessaly and Beotia; and as spring unlocked the ice
in torrents we halted to make shrines to Artemis and
Apollo, leaving wooden images behind us as protection.

 We had marched, ridden, sat and slept in rain
and sodden mud for weeks. A whole army
rotting for the sake of sisterhood. The Scythians
grumbled - being men they found the conditions

unbearable. But we fired them with thoughts
of rich pickings from the battlefield. Many Scythian
women had joined their men as foot soldiers.
They could be trusted to face the enemy with courage.

So steaming like a giant ox turd on the plain, our army
waited to engage in combat with Theseus' troops
which we did in the fourth month of that year. And fought
bravely until the seventh month when a truce was called.

THE SHAMAN

They were both gone to war, and there were years of living
still to accomplish – of waking each morning saddened
by dreams, pursued down days and nights by memories

of my child, Oreithyia; and Hippolyta her mother who was also
queen and priestess.The ache of separation was like losing
a limb. Yet traces of them spoke to me, in the evening wind

or in the growing light of morning – then they were with me
again, close and painful. The sound of water brought back the
days when I bathed Oreithyia in the oval copper tub. Her child's

hands flinging up drops like showers of gems. And later, riding
bareback on her fast Scythian ponies, their bridles glinting
with gold and silver cast into shapes of lions, eagles and buffalo

by the queen's own craftsmen, with a necklace of flowers, singing,
she raced past me; and I, her father, standing in the afternoon
shade with her spears and hunting dogs, basked in her glory.

I grew thin on memories, and the memories themselves
became weightless, uncertain. So, alone, I tried to keep
the faith while, far away, they fought their necessary battles.

THE MODERN WOMAN
Insight
31st March, 1985

Slowly sinking into sleep
I find myself on a pleasant hillside,
surrounded by scents of lavender
and roses – and the sound of bees
drowsing among warm flower borders.
It seems to me like those sacred
groves described by the poets,
Sappho and Erinna, where sandalled
girls tread lightly under boughs
of perfumed apple blossom,
walking on forest grasses moist with dew
and clean with the purity of an earlier creation.

It seems my goddesses are with me
on this hillside, with all those others in my life
that I have ever loved - all are gathered
for a moment like the briefest heartbeat,
yet eternal, bathed in light that shines
more kindly, surely, than the wavering beam
that chills our Northern altars when the old year
dies, and new comes squalling into being,
virgin birthed into the iron grave of winter.

THE AMAZON

We came over the ice
of the Cimmerian Bosphorous,
five thousand of us running in unison
at a steady pace, leaving freezing
trails of breath behind us.
We were robed in furs against
the bitterness of winter,
our minds and blades
sharpened for vengeance.
The blizzard rang against our shields
as we leaned heads down ·
into the blinding winds.

On our backs we carried staves,
ropes and rolls of canvas
for constructing rough shelters
when we stopped at night
to camp. Dog sleds flanked us
to the left and right, transporting
food, weapons and supplies
of the deadly poison with which
we tipped our arrows.
Those at the back carried spears,
knives and axes. In front, the archers
who could unleash winged death
in an instant. And all our strength
and all our javelins, and all our dreams
and lives were pledged to victory –
and keeping free

the spirit of the Amazons.

THE SHAMAN

To break her spirit they bound her and humbled her, then yoked
her to an ox and drove her naked through the city with other
captured
Amazons. Now crowds came not to marvel but to jeer at them.

For many years she lived in slavery in the household of Theseus –
cleaning and serving, measuring wine for the palace amphorae;
olive oil for use in the kitchens. For her it was a kind of death.

But she learned new skills – playing the lyre, inventing stories
for the women and children; the secret of making bistilla learned
from a Libyan cook – mincing tender pigeon with egg and herbs,

layering fine flakes of pastry into an airy castle that melts
against the palate. And at last, after many long years, she returned
to us, coming down the valley at dawn with her smooth, swift

stride. Not singing. She was dressed in simple clothes
like a goatherd. I walked out to greet her, slowly because
of my dim eyes and old bones. And slowly we came back

to the encampment surrounded by a ragged crowd of children
who had only ever heard her name in songs. Only knew her
by her reputation as first and best among athletes and warriors.

Oreithyia and I walked down to the river where her old pony
was tethered. After that tender reunion, I made us a soup of herbs
and onions which we ate with freshly baked bread. Then for days

and nights she slept on the bed of furs I made her in our wagon.
It was when she had recovered that she began to tell her story -
sitting by the camp fire at night with the wild dogs and owls and
stars

listening. Young and old alike sat wrapped in wonder as her thrilling
tales unfolded. My dreams tell me there will be no more war for us.
Other, stronger tribes will soon envelop us. But our songs and stories

will be remembered. Especially Oreithyia's story about the battle
to win which became in the end no more (or less) than a determination
to survive. And each day as she goes to meet her women friends

in their garden, I thank the gods and goddesses for giving me
this last gift for my old age. That I can love and care for my daughter
for a short time, at least, until we come to our final parting.

THE AMAZON

When the people heard news of our capture
they made a garden and each week planted
a new flower or fruit with which to honour us.
So those who fell in dust rose up each spring

again until there grew a vast army of stems
and stalks, of petals, blossoms, leaves and twigs,
plant, bushes, shrubs and trees.And those of us
still captive trained our minds only on that

garden where our names were spoken
every hour of every day by those who loved us.
And I, enslaved by Theseus and finding my
mother dead and my aunt, Antiope, worn down

by guilt and jealousy, had to hold hard to my
intended course which was to rescue Antiope
and escape. But when Theseus married the
Cretan princess Phaedra for her gold, Antiope

burst fully armed into the wedding feast and was
killed by guards. In the confusion afterwards,
I disguised myself as a goatherd, then picked up
my spears and arrows, and fled by night to freedom.

THE MODERN WOMAN
The Way to Freedom
6th April, 1985

The arrows point to EXIT – the way to freedom –
beyond the ward and the car park. A new life.
And He tells me – the One in the white coat
that is – to find a new path to follow.

"Avoid stress," he says. "Or find better ways
to deal with it." And "Do things you want to do –
things that make you happy." But his meter is running.
Another patient waiting. I close his door behind me

and notice spears of sunlight piercing the dark
hospital corridor. Birds swoop outside the window.
A swordthrust of hunger reminds me the troops
need feeding if I'm going to win any battles.

So I forget the weekly shop and head
for a pub lunch – past a battleaxe of an orderly
and battalions of sad people shuffling towards
appointments. And I think of the one-breasted

Amazons; fellow women yet brave and practical
about their own survival who harnessed their energies
into living and dying with courage. And, suddenly,
I know that's what I want to do too.

So I follow the arrows.

Epilogue

If You Must Go Into The Starless Night Alone

If you must go into the starless night alone,
have courage – we are with you; not angels,
saints or martyrs but ordinary women,
honouring kindness, mindful of the needs
of others. Our thoughts cradle the world,
comfort history against the shadow of chaos.

You'll throw off your coverlet of snowdrop
and primrose, run barefoot across the grass –
a child again, released into morning, into birdsong.

You'll hear the murmur of voices
like bees drowsing on the warm hillside –
follow the sound through the old garden,
past walls heavy with apricots; you'll inhale
scents of roses and lavender, just as we did.

Soon you'll find us, leaning on our spears,
facing the dawn – a brave tribe with our
wounds and battlescars; warriors, athletes,
poets, scholars – travellers in mind and body,
resting for a moment between journeys.

When you are refreshed, it'll be time to move on;
to venture out once more across the vast, cloudy
universe – solitary spirit, yet part of a thousand
indomitable armies whose voices you've heard calling,
telling you when it's time to leave, or to come, home.

IRON Press was formed in Spring 1973, initially to publish the magazine IRON which more than two decades, and more than 1,500 writers on, survives as one of the country's most active alternative mags – a fervent purveyor of new poetry, fiction and graphics. £14.00 gets you a subscription. Try our intriguing book list too, titles which can rarely be found on the shelves of mega-stores. Fortified by a belief in good writing, as against literary competitions or marketing trivia, IRON remains defiantly a small press. Our address is at the front of this book.